Earwitness

OTHER BOOKS BY ELIAS CANETTI

EARWITNESS

Fifty Characters

ELIAS CANETTI

Translated from the German by
JOACHIM NEUGROSCHEL

A *Continuum Book*
THE SEABURY PRESS · NEW YORK

1979 · The Seabury Press
815 Second Avenue · New York, N.Y. 10017

Originally published as *Der Ohrenzeuge: Fünfzig Charaktere* by Carl Hanser Verlag,
copyright © 1974 by Carl Hauser Verlag, München
English translation copyright © 1979 by The Seabury Press, Inc.

Printed in the United States of America

Library of Congress Cataloging in Publication Data

Canetti, Elias, 1905–
Earwitness.

(A Continuum book)
Translation of Der Ohrenzeuge.
I. Title.
PT2605.A580413   833'.9'12   78-31192
ISBN 0-8164-9357-X

For Hera and Johanna

Characters

The King-proclaimer

The king-proclaimer has something majestic about her, she realizes what she owes to her mission and is known for her fine treatment of guests. But there is more to it than hospitality, and everyone senses that something special is in the offing. She does not say right off what it will be this time, it heightens the suspense. It cannot be under a king, she never proclaims less. She is tall and stately, and her supply of scorn is inexhaustible. She can tell underlings by the least gesture and keeps them away from the king before he is even proclaimed. But she has a good eye for courtiers too, she knows how to skillfully advance their careers and uses them for all courts. One can sense the way she gathers her exuberance and reserves it for the grand occasion. She is harsh and despises beggars, unless they present themselves when they are needed. She pays her respects with a whole score of them when the king is about to be proclaimed. Then all the doors in her house fly open, it expands into a palace, angels sing, bishops bless, in her new vestments she reads a telegram from God and jubilantly proclaims the king.

It is touching to see her with forgotten kings, she never forgets them, she retains even the worst has-beens among them, writes to them, sends them suitable small gifts, obtains work for them, and when the honor is long past, she is the only person still to remember it. Among the beggars with whom she pays her respects on grand occasions, one can find a former king or two.

The Name-licker

The name-licker knows what is good, he can smell it a thousand miles away and spares no effort to get near the name that he plans to lick. Nowadays that is an easy matter by car or by plane, the effort is not all that great, but it must be said that he would make more of an effort if it were necessary. His cravings arise when he reads the newspapers, anything that is not in the newspapers is not his cup of tea. If a name recurs frequently in the newspapers and even appears in the headlines, his craving becomes irresistible and he hastily gets underway. If he has enough money for the trip, then fine; if he does not, he borrows it and pays with the glory of his grand goal. It always makes an impression when he speaks about it. "I have to lick N.N.," he says, and it sounds as the discovery of the North Pole once sounded.

He knows how to pay a surprise visit whether citing someone else or not, he always sounds as though he were about to perish. It flatters names that a craving for them could make someone die of thirst, the whole world a desert and they the only well. And so, not without first complaining in detail about their lack of time, they agree to receive the name-licker. One might even say that they wait for him somewhat impatiently. They put their best parts aright for him, wash them— and only them—thoroughly and polish them to a high shine. The name-licker appears and is dazzled. Meanwhile his lust has grown and he does not hide it. He walks up impudently and seizes the name. After licking and licking it thoroughly, he photographs it. He has nothing to say, perhaps he stammers something that sounds like veneration, but no one falls for it, they know that all he cares about is the contact of his tongue. "With my very own tongue," he announces later on, sticking it out and receiving an awe such as has never been imparted to any name.

The Submitter

The submitter has plans in his briefcase, appeals, drawings and figures. He is quite at home in them, he sprang into life ready-made from his briefcase. He was never conceived, no mother ever carried him, he was always able to read and count. He was never a child prodigy because he was never a child. He never grows older because he was never younger: his planification is devoid of years. He is punctual without noticing it. He is never early and he is never late, but if you ask him what time it is he strikes his head at such utter stupidity.

It does not matter to him that his submitting is gratuitous, and when he comes for signatures for a good cause, he always has a few to show, they may be viewed. How he ever acquired them is a mystery, he is silent, he has his methods. He is patient and has been submitting the same things for years. His briefcase is full and variety is certain. No one notices when he comes with the same thing because the last time was too long ago. He remembers everything for he carries it around with him, it is part of his character as a submitter never to give up anything. He insists on persuasion, he allows no one to sign unless the person in question understands him thoroughly. He is always looking for names but he wants them totally; once he has someone in his briefcase, that person has to stay there. He despises people who abscond from his briefcase, very few succeed. He holds them up as warning examples and keeps on submitting.

He gets nothing out of it himself, he does it all for free. He implies that he hardly needs anything for himself and will not even let someone treat him to a cup of coffee. Sometimes he is called for by another submitter, like a twin, but their names are different. When they leave together, you cannot tell which of them was here first. Perhaps they ultimately catch up with their origins and turn into eggs after a period of submitting.

The Self-giver

She lives from the presents that she takes back. She never forgets a present. She knows all of them, she remembers where each one is. She combs all areas for them and always finds pretexts. She likes to enter unfamiliar houses, hoping to find a present from herself there too. Even withered flowers blossom again in order to let her take them back.

How could she ever have given so many presents and how could she have failed to get them back earlier. She, who forgets everything, never forgets presents, and her only problem is presents that have been eaten up. It's painful when she appears and everything has been consumed. She then sits there pensive and bewildered, recalling something that ought to be there. She peers around furtively, a polite woman, wondering if something might be hidden. She particularly loves going into kitchens, a glance at the garbage, a jolt in her heart, there they are, the peels of her oranges. If only she had brought them later or had come for them earlier.

"My teapot!" she says and collects it. "My scarf! My flowers! My blouse!" If the recipient is wearing the blouse, she asks her if she might try it on and, not without first admiring herself from all sides in the mirror, she leaves, still wearing the blouse.

7

But doesn't she expect her recipients to bring the presents back on their own? No, she prefers getting them herself. But does she help herself to anything? No, all she cares about is her presents. She dotes on them, she wants them, they belong to her. But why did she give them away? In order to get them back, that was why she gave them away.

The Tattletale

The tattletale won't keep anything to himself if it could hurt someone's feelings. He hurries and gets a steal on other tattletales. Sometimes it is a bitter race, and even though not all of them start at the same point, he can sense how close the others are already and he outstrips them in gigantic leaps. He speaks very fast and it is a secret. No one must find out that he knows. He expects gratitude, and it consists in discretion. "I'm only telling you. It concerns only you." The tattletale knows when a position is threatened. Since he moves so quickly—he is very hurried—the threat grows en route. He arrives, and everything is safe and sure. "You're being dismissed." The victim blanches. "When?" he asks. And, "How can that be? No one's said anything to me." "It's being kept a secret. They're going to tell you at the very last moment. I had to warn you. But don't give me away." Then he gives a detailed speech on how awful it would be if he were given away, and before the victim even has time to fully gauge the danger he's in, he already feels sorry for the tattletale, that best friend of his.

The tattletale will overlook no insult uttered in anger, and he makes sure that it reaches the insultee. He is less anxious to carry back praise, but to show his good will, he occasionally forces himself to do so. In such cases, he never hurries, he tarries where he is. Praise lies on his tongue like unsavory poison.

9

Before spitting it out, he feels as if he were choking. Finally he speaks it, but very chastely, as though timid at the other man's nakedness.

Otherwise he knows neither shame nor disgust. "You've got to defend yourself. You've got to do something! You can't just take it sitting down!" He likes to counsel the victim, if for no other reason than because it takes longer. His advice is such that it magnifies the victim's fear. After all, the only thing the tattletale cares about is other people's confidence, he cannot live without confidence.

The Tear-warmer

The tear-warmer goes to the movies every day. It doesn't always have to be something new, he is also drawn to old films, all that counts is that they fulfill their purpose and elicit tears galore from him. You sit in the darkness, unseen by others, and wait for fulfillment. The world is cold and heartless, and a man wouldn't care to live without feeling the warm wetness on his cheeks. As soon as the tears begin to pour, you feel good, you are very still and you don't move a muscle, you wouldn't dream of wiping anything away with your handkerchief, each tear has to bestow its warmth down to the very lees, and whether it gets to the mouth or the chin, or whether it actually succeeds in running over the throat all the way down to the chest—he accepts it with thankful restraint and gets up again only after a good bath.

The tear-warmer was not always so well off, there were times when he was dependent on his own misfortune, and if it didn't come and kept him waiting, he often felt as if he were about to freeze to death. He twisted about in life uncertainly, towards a loss, a hurt, an inconsolable grief. But people do not always die when you want to be sad, most of them have their tenacious lives and they balk. At times, he was all set for a moving experience, his limbs were already beginning to let go pleasurably. But then—he thought he was right on the verge—then, nothing happened, he had wasted too much

11

time, and he had to look around for a new opportunity and start all over again with his expectation.

It took the tear-warmer many disappointments to realize that no man has enough unhappiness in his own life to get his money's worth. He tried any number of things, he even tried joys. But anyone at all versed in that area knows that tears of joy do not go very far. Even if they fill up the eyes, as sometimes happens—they do not really get flowing, and as for the permanence of their effect, it is a rather lamentable affair. Nor do fury and anger prove to be any more productive. There is only one cause to be counted on: losses, whereby the irrevocable kind are preferable to all the rest, especially when happening to people who do not deserve them.

The tear-warmer has a long apprenticeship behind him but now he is a past master. Anything not granted to him he gets from others. If these people do not concern him at all, strange, remote, beautiful, innocent, great, the effect increases ad infinitum. He himself, however, suffers no damage, he leaves the movie house and calmly goes home. Here, everything is as usual, he is not concerned about anything, and the next day will bring him no worries.

The Blind Man

The blind man is not blind by birth, but he became blind with little effort. He has a camera, he takes it everywhere, and he just loves keeping his eyes closed. He walks about as though asleep, he has seen absolutely nothing as yet, and already he is shooting it, for when all things lie next to one another, equally small, equally large, always rectangular, orderly, cut off, named, numbered, proven, and demonstrated, then you can see them much better in any event.

The blind man saves himself the trouble of viewing anything beforehand. He gathers the things he would have seen and piles them up and enjoys them as though they were stamps. He travels all over the world for the sake of his camera, nothing is far enough, shiny enough, strange enough—he gets it for the camera. He says: I was there, and he points to it, and if he could not point at it he would not know where he had been, the world is confusing, exotic, and rich, who can retain it all?

The blind man does not believe anything that was not shot. People chatter and boast and talk through their hats, his motto is: Get out the photos! Then you know what a man has really seen, then you hold it hard in your hand, then you can put your finger on it, then you can also calmly open your eyes instead of senselessly squandering them beforehand. Every-

13

thing in life has its season, too much is too much, save your eyesight for photos.

The blind man loves to project enlargements of his photos on the wall and treat his friends to the show. Such a festival lasts two or three hours, silence, explanations, indications, interpretations, advice, humor. The jubilation when something has been inserted upside down, the *savoir-faire* when you realize that something is being shown for the second time! There is no saying how good a man feels when the shots are big and the show goes on long enough. At last the reward for the unswerving blindness of a whole trip. Open up, open up, you eyes, now you may see, now it's time, now you've been there, now you have to prove it.

The blind man is sorry that other people can also prove it, but he proves it better.

The Long-changer

The long-changer gives more than he gets. He knows more and has more than anyone else. He saddles a burglar with so much that the man collapses under the load. Then he helps him carry it downstairs. Then he shows him the way and warns him of dangers.

The long-changer has meticulous conversations with specialists. He advises all of them, is there anything he does not know, he knows more than any of them. No one understands where he gets the time to read, and can a man read about everything today? He can, or else it comes to him in his sleep, he has an airtight memory. He does not say "I know," for he knows a lot more, but he does say instantly what he knows more, he says it matter-of-factly and beneficially, he is not arrogant, he is actually modest, but he also gives more than he gets, he is like a mysteriously constructed vending machine.

The long-changer frequents all circles, he makes no distinction among them, he is no snob and will not deny himself to anybody. Nor does he want to be considered a do-gooder. His outer appearance is inconspicuous, he never looks out of the ordinary, he does not lurk, he walks, stands, sits, and turns like anyone else. Some people see him as a running bird, but not an especially large one. He smiles when receiving something but is deadly serious when giving. His ears are pointed

15

and lean slightly forward. He keeps his tongue well-hidden, whatever he says is said with a secret tongue.

When the long-changer simply will not stop talking anymore, people know he is asleep. He no longer hears then, he gives incessantly then, he gets absolutely nothing then, he is happy then.

The Narrow-smeller

The narrow-smeller shrinks away from smells and avoids them. She opens doors cautiously, hesitating before she crosses a threshold. Half-averted, she stands there for a while, to smell with one nostril and spare the other. She sticks one finger into the unknown space and brings it to her nose. Then, with that finger, she holds one nostril shut and sniffs with the other. If she does not lose consciousness immediately, she waits a bit. Then she puts one leg sideways across the threshold, but leaves the other foot outside. It would not take much more for her to dare it, but she hits upon a final test in time. She gets up on her tiptoes and sniffs again. If the smell does not change now, she fears no surprises and risks the other leg as well. She is standing inside. The door, through which she could save herself, remains wide open.

The narrow-smeller seems isolated wherever she may be, she has a layer of caution about her; other people watch out for their clothes when they sit down, but she watches out for her isolation layer. She fears vehement sentences that might pierce through, she addresses people softly and awaits answers just as softly. She does not come halfway to anyone; in the aloofness in which she remains, she follows the movements of other people: It is as though, separated from them, she were constantly dancing with them. The distance remains the same, she knows how to ward off any approach and certainly any touch.

So long as it is winter, the narrow-smeller feels best out of doors. She worries about the spring. The blossoms and fragrances will begin and she will suffer unbearable torments. She prudently avoids certain bushes, she goes her own, intricate ways. When she sees an insensitive person sticking his nose in lilacs far away, she becomes ill. Unfortunately, she is attractive and gets pursued with roses, she can save herself from them only with quick faints. People find this exaggerated, and while she dreams about distilled water, her admirers put their foul-reeking heads together and try to figure out to which flower scents they could convert her.

The narrow-smeller is regarded as noble because she avoids any touch. She is at her wits' end with marriage proposals. She has already threatened to hang herself. But she will not do it, she cannot bear the thought of possibly having to smell the savior who cuts her down.

The Goods-and-chattels

The goods-and-chattels likes to have everything together, close at hand. She does not spread out, she remains where she is, she wants to have a clear view of her property. A thing need not be large, even small things have their value if they are always within reach. She is cautious and tender with money, never spending more than one tenth and taking care of the rest. She feeds her money so that it won't perish. She never takes a morsel of food without leaving some of it for her money.

It is touching to see the way the goods-and-chattels ties a napkin around her money before a meal. She does not like it to get dirty, she likes it to be clean. Of course she does get some bills that are not new. But under her care, they are transformed and become radiant as on the first day. At times, she arranges the individual bills next to one another on the table, like a large, well-mannered family, and she gives them names. Then she counts to check whether they are all still there, and when they have eaten like good little things, she puts them to bed.

The goods-and-chattels takes tiny steps between the chest and the bed, carrying something that she removes from one and puts in the other. She likes to apply the dust cloth, but not too much, you have to give things time, value goes up with time, it would be nice to have a lot of time. The goods-

19

and-chattels imagines what value everything will have by the time she celebrates her eightieth birthday. She studies prices and questions her son, he visits her once a month. For these visits, she prepares everything and arranges it properly so that she can use every minute of the visit. There are so many questions one would like to ask, no sooner is he gone than they come to mind, so it is better to think everything out beforehand.

The goods-and-chattels does not associate with neighbors. They only wear out the threshold and snoop around, no sooner are they in the room than something is already gone. You can look for it all you like till it pops up again. She does not mean to say that everyone is a thief, goodness, but the objects are afraid of strangers and creep away, and if they did not hide out so well—who knows if they were not stolen.

The goods-and-chattels receives mail and lets it lie for a few days without opening it. She puts such a letter on the table in front of her and imagines that it contains a great deal more. She is also a bit afraid that it is less, but since that has never happened and since everything goes up with time, she can wait and hope that it is more.

The Corpse-skulker

Now and then, the corpse-skulker appears in a bar. He's been known here for years, but he doesn't come often. If people don't see him for a few months, they wonder about him, slightly worried. He always carries a bag from some airline, Air France or BEA. He seems to travel a great deal, since he often vanishes for such long stretches. He is always back again in the same way. He appears and halts earnestly in the doorway. He scours the bar, looking for acquaintances. The moment he spots one, he walks over solemnly, greets him, stops, remains silent, and then says in a lamenting, rather singsong voice: "Have you heard, N. N. has died." The acquaintance is startled, for he did not know, and the corpse-skulker is wearing black, which you only notice after his announcement. "The funeral is tomorrow." He invites you to the funeral, he explains where it is, and gives detailed and precise directions. "Do come," he adds. "You won't regret it."

Then he sits down, orders a drink, toasts your health, says a few words, never tells where he has been, never tells what his plans are, he gets up, walks solemnly to the door, turns around once more, says "Tomorrow at eleven," and vanishes.

Thus he goes from bar to bar, looking for acquaintances, who were also acquaintances of the deceased, he makes sure that there are not too few of them, he infects them with his funeral lusts and invites them so emphatically that some people come even though they would never have dreamt of it, but fearing his next announcement could be about them.

The Fame-tester

Since his birth, the fame-tester has known that nobody could be better than he. He may have known it earlier, but he could not say so back then. Now he is eloquent and tries to show how awful the world is. Every day he skims through the newspapers, looking for new names, what's this one doing there, he shouts indignantly, it wasn't there yesterday! There's something fishy going on, how can anybody suddenly sneak into the papers? He grabs it between his thumb and forefinger, sticks it between his teeth, and bites. It is incredible how woefully the new stuff yields. Ugh! Wax! And it thinks it's metal!

It gives him no peace, he investigates the matter, he is a fair man; if there is *anything* he takes seriously, it is the public, he won't be taken in by fraudulent practices and he'll show that dirty new name a thing or two. From the first moment of discovery, he follows every stirring of that scum. Here he has said something wrong and there he can't spell. Where did he go to school anyway? Did he really go to college or is he simply pretending? Why didn't he ever get married? And what does he do in his spare time? How come no one ever heard of him? The old days lasted long enough, and where was he then? If he's old, it certainly took him a long time; if he's young, then he ought to get his diapers washed. The fame-tester looks him up in all available reference books but, to his satisfaction, he finds him nowhere.

One may say that the fame-tester lives with the deceiver, he talks and dreams about him incessantly. He feels pestered by him and persecuted, and he stubbornly refuses to fill out a good-conduct certificate for him. When he comes home and finally wants his peace, he deposits him in a corner and says: "Down boy!" and threatens him with a whip. But the sly new name is patient and waits. He exudes a peculiar smell, and when the fame-tester is asleep, the smell cuts into his nose.

The Beauty-newt

The beauty-newt, called bewt for short by some people, is keen on all the beautiful things that have existed, do exist, or will exist in the world, and he finds them in palaces, museums, temples, churches, and caves. It does not trouble him that something considered beautiful for a long time has become slightly rancid for that very reason, for him it remains what it always was, even though new beauties are being added daily, each one is beautiful in its own right, none excludes the rest, each can expect him to stand adoringly before it and admire it. One need merely see him in front of the Sistine Madonna or the Naked Maja, approaching from various sides, stopping at various distances, lingering for a long time, or else a short time, with rich variety, and regretting any impossibility of approaching from behind.

The beauty-newt or bewt makes sure to speak no words that might be detrimental to his adoration. He opens himself up wide and goes mute, he does not compare, he does not nit-pick, he does not refer to periods, styles, and customs. He does not want to know how the beauty inventor felt and most certainly not what he thought. Each one lived somehow or other, it does not matter whether it was hard, and it could not have been too hard, otherwise the beautiful would not exist now, the very fact that he bore it within him was fortunate, and made him enviable, if these subjective trivia were of interest.

25

Personally, the bewt is doing just fine; privately, he has no trouble finding and dedicating himself to beauties. He is careful not to buy them so as not to be partisan, and besides, it would be a hopeless undertaking, for most beauties are in firm hands. The money he has is unimportant, he uses it economically for his nonstop traveling. He vanishes on trips, one never sees him en route, it is as though he traveled invisibly. To make up for it, he makes an appearance before the beauties, and once you have seen him in Arezzo or the Brera, you will be sure to see him again in Borobudur and Nara.

The bewt is ugly, everyone avoids him, it would be ungentlemanly to describe his repulsive looks. Let it be said that he never had a nose. His pop eyes, his jughandle ears, his goiter, his black, rotten teeth, the pestilential stench he exudes from his mouth, his sometimes squeaky, sometimes croaking voice, his doughy hands—who cares, who cares, since he never holds them out to anyone and unerringly finds his place in front of all beauties?

The Man-splendid Woman

The man-splendid woman is a curve-blossom and likes to stand up. There she stands, slowly lifting her arm aloft and holding it aloft with a carefully studied gesture. When all the onlookers close their dazzled eyes, she drops her arm, somewhat more swiftly. Then she gazes into the distance as though no one were present, turns around 180 degrees, lifts her other arm even more slowly, and, lost in thought, she fingers her hairdo, which is no less *soigné* than her shoulders.

She does not say a word, what could she say anyway to heighten her splendor, she holds her tongue, and her silence speaks volumes. Privately, her name is Mrs. Shouldershine, what name was ever more appropriate. No matter where she is, among people or at home, she never tires of standing there (what a figure!) and lifting now her left and now her right arm. It must be emphasized that she does the same thing at home, alone at her mirror.

She does it for herself, she has said, her only recorded sentence, it takes a good deal of presumptuousness to describe her as the man-splendid woman. During the day, she is calm, she can stand and incessantly delight in her lifted arms. At night, it is harder, she does not always dream about herself and she does not like to forget herself. So she sleeps fitfully, she sleeps with the light on. From time to time, she awakes, she glides

27

from her bed—she already sees herself, she already lifts her arm, her shoulder already shines, she already gazes into the distance. Then, halfway calm again, she goes back to bed. If that is not enough for her, the other arm takes its turn.

Can anyone be surprised that many men are after her shoulders? She, however, notices none of them; she is immune, can she help it if men misinterpret her splendor? Something that exists for its own sake is seen by them as existing for them, is it the fault of the man-splendid woman that she is built like that? She has to watch out for her complexion, and love is not good for it. Perfection belongs to no one and requires distance, that, and that alone, is why she stares into the distance.

Mrs. Shouldershine lives alone and will not have a lapdog or a cat; after all, they would not grasp who she is; a child would be inconceivable, she would have to bend over for it. Even if she lifted it up, it still could not see her, and what would it understand about her stunning parts? She is doomed to live alone, she takes her fate courageously upon herself, and no one, no one, has ever heard a complaint from her lips.

The Damage-fresh Man

The damage-fresh man has a wry face and a nasal twang. He cares little for people and seeks proof. He knows people only if something goes awry for them. He is not content with illnesses, which are too frequent, accidents are somewhat better. If they lead to serious injuries, he livens up, there is no detail that he then lets pass, the worse the outcome, the better for him. He listens to it, does not shake his head, asks and asks, and likes to be taken to the scenes of accidents. The event is reconstructed, and as unavoidable as it was, it was still always the fault of the victim. The damage-fresh man needs misfortune, it is heavenly manna for him, he feels fine so long as he learns enough about other people's misfortunes, if he has heard nothing for a long time, he shrinks and parches up.

He can smell the painful end in anything told to him. He never warns about it, he takes care not to. He is of the persuasion that people should be on their own, anyone who butts in and gives advice will draw the misfortune upon himself; he knows of only *one* way to get through life, namely to let it take its course.

The damage-fresh man is respectful of events. Things come as they come, only weaklings look away, a man looks every misfortune of others courageously in the eye. Anything that does not happen to him proves his discernment. One can

29

scarcely believe how much misfortune can be gotten from the world, one eye searches for it in this direction, the other in that direction. His restraint, when he has once again gotten a whiff of something, is exercised in his nasal twang.

The damage-fresh man regards himself as immune because his eyes never find any rest. With other people's misfortunes he eludes anything that could threaten him personally. No sooner has something happened, than the next thing happens, there is simply no time for something to happen to him. He likes to say, "It had to happen!" And he also likes to say, "Not me!" The damage-fresh man won't be put off with newspapers. Only when nothing proper has happened for a long time, when he feels the dry spell reaching around him—only then, and not without reluctance, will he take a juicy catastrophe in hand and indulge in details that were not communicated to him personally.

The Culprit

The culprit admits to every crime under the sun. Whether she hears about it, or reads it in the newspaper, she instantly recognizes what she has done and hangs her head. She broods about it, trying to determine how it was possible, how could she forget such a dreadful thing. She would never have dreamt of it, she had no idea, that very morning, when getting up, she was preoccupied with a totally different crime, her previous one. But as soon as the new one was articulated, as soon as she read about it, it struck her with a certainty that shoved all earlier things aside, and now she has only this one thought.

The only right thing would be to give herself up on the spot, go to the police and make a detailed confession. But she has had some bad experiences in that area; policemen, as she has come to realize only too well, know absolutely nothing about human nature. All she need do is open her mouth, and they consider her innocent. Those people don't even truly listen to her, they interrupt, and amiably say: "Really?" and send her home. It is as though the laws did not apply to her. She has tried petitions and has anticipated the solution to several crimes by immediately pointing out the culprit: herself. She is never at a loss for details to corroborate her statement: the instant she knows she has done it, she develops a stupendous memory. But other people always succeed in pushing their way in and usurping the blame. She absolutely cannot

31

stand reading about the horrible trials in which others, in her stead, are punished with prison or penitentiary. She is ashamed of the state of the penal system, which utterly ignores her, since she would always be prepared to atone for her misdeed. How much money is thrown out on investigations, what extravagance, what long and drawn-out procedures! What ever do they think, those fools who ultimately confess, what kind of mental aberration can that be, forcing them to admit to something they could not possibly have done?

Sometimes when she is so confused by such events in the world that she cannot regain her bearings, she wonders whether one and the same crime might conceivably be committed twice? Could all others be fools and she the only clear-sighted person? She certainly has no illusions about herself, God forbid, how could a person capable of such a thing suffer from illusions. But it is indeed bizarre how little most people know about themselves.

The culprit does not break down. She keeps a grip on herself, she gathers her strength, she lives for the day when she will get justice. Crimes come, crimes go, but then, once she is recognized, she will stand there with her head raised high and gratefully accept the punishment that is her due.

The Misspeaker

The misspeaker, when he wishes to speak, looks for people who do not know what he is talking about. He knows the bewildered look, the helpless blinking, when he addresses someone, and he throws himself into his speech only when the blinking is helpless enough. Ideas galore come pouring in, arguments that would never have occurred to him are available now in abundance; he feels he can confuse everyone now, his mood heightens to the darkest inspiration, the atmosphere around him is alive with oracles.

But alas and alack, if the other man's face twitches, as with sudden insight, with understanding—then the misspeaker goes into a slump, gets muddled, stammers, falters, tries again in the most awkward embarrassment, and when he realizes that it's all for nothing, that the other man understands and is determined to persevere in his understanding, then the misspeaker gives up, goes mute, and brusquely turns away.

Such defeats are not frequent, however. Usually the misspeaker succeeds in not being understood. He is experienced and selective, he does not talk to just anyone. He knows the type of people who grasp anything. As though anybody could have a clue of what he meant to say! He himself does not know in advance; what he is about to say is written nowhere, not even in the stars, how can anyone else know it? The misspeaker senses that inspiration is blind. Inspiration can be kindled only by nothing. It would be easy to start with the confusion in which lower natures indulge. He bears the world as chaos inside himself. Chaos is innate in him, it chooses a bearer once in a hundred years: him.

One could assume the most sublime thing for him would be to settle matters himself with chaos. One pictures the misspeaker talking only to himself. But that is an unforgivable error. The misspeaker can be sparked only by the obstinacy of others. In this densely populated city, he walks up and down and around in a circle, stopping in front of this man or that man, throwing out a pointless lure, observing his effect, and it is only when perceiving the desired bafflement that he starts blazing away and is elevated to his chaos.

The Tablecloth-lunatic

The tablecloth-lunatic is dazzling white and breathes in linen. Her fingers are strict, her eyes angular. As far back as she can remember, she has never had a cold, and yet her voice is slightly hoarse. She says she has never had a dream, and people believe her.

Some people come to her to get order. She is irresistible. She says little, but whatever she says has the dogmatic force of an entire church. It is not certain that she prays, she is her own church. When she celebrates the dazzling white, one is plunged into shame for living so long in filth. Compared with her, everything is filth, denials are futile. She opens her angular eyes wide, trains them undimmed on someone, and one senses a radiance from within. It is as though one had all her tablecloths inside, strictly folded, never spread, on a dazzling white heap, forever, forever.

But she is never fully satisfied, for even she finds spots in the dazzlement. One ought to see her when she unexpectedly stops short upon noticing a tiny dot. Now she turns dangerous, like a poisonous snake. Now she opens her mouth and shows dreadful fangs. Now she hisses before striking, the tiny spot takes its life into its hands. At times, it was so frightened of her that it vanished and she hunted it doggedly for hours on end. But at other times, it does not vanish. The result is a hurricane. She grabs the dazzling white, she does not grab it alone, she grabs it together with twenty other dazzling whites, where it was stacked and she sets about rewashing the entire lofty pack at once.

At such moments, one is well-advised to leave her in peace, for her fury knows no limits. Anything within reach is also washed. Tables, chairs, beds, people, animals. It is like the Last Judgment. Now nothing finds grace in her angular eyes. Now animals and people have already been washed to death. Now it is like the time before the Creation of all beings. Now light and darkness are separated. Now God is no longer sure of what to do next.

The Water-harborer

The water-harborer lives in fear that he is bound to die of thirst and so he collects water. His wine cellar looks well-stocked, but it is no wine cellar, all the bottles are filled with water, sealed by him personally, and arranged by year.

The water-harborer is racked by the waste of water. That's how it started on the moon. "Water? Why save water? We've got enough from here to eternity!" So they left the faucets half-open, they kept dripping, people took a bath every day. That was a frivolous breed up there. And what became of them? When the first reports of the moon arrived, the water-harborer was beside himself with excitement. He had always known it was because of the water, the men on the moon died out because of the way they wasted water. He had said so everywhere, and people laughed and thought he was crazy. But now, now they had been up there, and they could see in black and white, even in color. Not a drop of water and no human being anywhere! It was not hard putting two and two together.

The water-harborer saves early. He goes to neighbors and asks for some water. They are glad to oblige, he comes again. He thereby spares his own faucet, which shares his sensitivity and closes up before it is too late. Anything they give him he puts in a safe place, not a single drop is lost en route. The bottles are lying ready in the kitchen, the labels with the year written on them, the wax for sealing. Actually, this is no longer a kitchen, you would have to call it a water studio. He already has fine reserves, and if worst comes to worst, he and his family could manage for a while. But he doesn't speak about it, he's afraid of burglars, and feels it is wiser to keep silent about his rich cellar.

The water-harborer cries when it rains. Today was the Last Time, he whispers, we will remember this day for a long time. It does rain again, but he, a counter of drops, knows that there is less rain each time, soon it will stop altogether, the children will ask: What was rain like; and adults will have a hard time explaining it to them in the prevailing drought.

The Early Worder

The early worder speaks on ice skates and outstrips pedestrians. The words drop from his mouth like empty hazelnuts. They are light, being empty, but there are many of them. There is one with meat for every thousand empty ones, but that is mere chance. The early worder says nothing he has thought over, he says it beforehand. It is not his heart that runneth over, but the tip of his tongue. Nor does it matter what he says, so long as he starts. His blinking is a signal that it will go on, it is not yet over, then he blinks again and keeps blinking until the other man gives up all hope and listens.

The early worder does not lower himself to sit down, that would be a slow affair, he would rather frolic around skating rinks, which are bright and smooth and where others of his ilk hastily admire him. He avoids darkness. He swallows the newspaper. He reads it as though personally speaking it, so fast, it is already transformed into his words, it tumbles out of his mouth and reports on yesterday and the day after tomorrow. He has an easy time with time; while other people struggle under its weight, he has gotten over and ahead of time and never takes a breath to catch his breath. So it does not really matter what newspaper he reads, he pulls one from every pile, none is old, so long as it is a different one, and all the headlines are easy to transpose.

39

The early worder has never changed, for nothing sticks to him. He is instantly rid of people and clothes: without quite noticing it, he gets to others; and as for people, they all have first names that are repeated. If things do not work without names, he uses any old name and is already blinking as soon as he has spoken it, people think he is joking and no one gets around to asking.

The early worder has people of his own for practice. They are no different for him than anyone else is, yet he is somewhat bothered that they are not quite new. He would much prefer being able to trade them in for others, and then do the same with these, and so on and on, for they are much too keen on being known to him and readily misuse a moment to open their mouths and say something.

The Syllable-pure Woman

The syllable-pure woman has a golden scale, she removes it from her bag and puts it aside. Then she takes a word from her mouth and quickly lays it on the scale. She knows its weight from before, but she has a fastidious conscience. She will not use the word before weighing it. She makes sure that every syllable pulls its own weight and she takes care that none is swallowed. When each syllable lies in its place, not too wide, not too narrow, clearly outlined and without airs, she nods and grants herself permission to read off the total weight of the word. It scarcely changes, but the confirmation decides. Words whose weight vacillates too much will not pass her lips.

The syllable-pure woman speaks so unshakably correctly that others listen to her with open mouths. Perhaps they hope to swallow the words themselves and keep them for the right moment. Absurd hope! Words do not fit into every mouth, they bounce back from some like marbles. It is gratifying to know that they cannot be held where they do not feel suitable. Syllable-pure people are rare and can be counted on the fingers of one hand. A life of self-denial is required, and an incorruptible attitude. Such a person must know how to keep words unalloyed and never misuse them for selfish ends. It does not matter what one says, but it must be said purely. The safest thing is being content to say nothing with pure words.

41

The syllable-pure woman sometimes takes hold of a book merely to inspect it. If there are words that are not fully lost, she detaches them from their degenerate milieu and places them in a golden vat. There she cleanses them carefully with noble acids, and when all traces of their besmirchment are gone, she plucks them out with ice-cooled tweezers, carries them to a wellspring those waters have been tested, and she lets them lie there in the moonlight for seven nights. It has to be an out-of-the-way wellspring so that the process of purification will not be disturbed by nature freaks.

The syllable-pure woman has a mouth in which words do not fester. Supposedly, she never uses it for eating, so as not to endanger her protégés. She feeds on aromatic liquids, which are beneficial to them. Her life is virginal like that of a vestal. Yet this holy life is not difficult for her: she lives it in honor of speech as speech ought to be; and so long as the scale and the vat are golden, she remains undaunted and will not be thwarted by any gross corrupter.

The Earwitness

The earwitness makes no effort to look, but he hears all the better. He comes, halts, huddles unnoticed in a corner, peers into a book or a display, hears whatever is to be heard, and moves away untouched and absent. One would think he was not there for he is such an expert at vanishing. He is already somewhere else, he is already listening again, he knows all the places where there is something to be heard, stows it nicely away, and forgets nothing.

He forgets nothing, one has to watch the earwitness when it is time for him to come out with everything. At such a time, he is another man, he is twice as large and four inches taller. How does he do it, does he have special high shoes for blurting things out? Could he possibly pad himself with pillows to make his words seem heavier and weightier? He does nothing else, he says it very precisely, some people wish they had held their tongues. All those modern gadgets are superfluous: his ear is better and more faithful than any gadget, nothing is erased, nothing is blocked, no matter how bad it is, lies, curses, four-letter words, all kinds of indecencies, invectives from remote and little-known languages, he accurately registers even things he does not understand and delivers them unaltered if people wish him to do so.

The earwitness cannot be corrupted by anybody. When it comes to this useful gift, which he alone has, he would take no heed of wife, child, or brother. Whatever he has heard, he has heard, and even the Good Lord is helpless to change it. But he also has human sides, and just as others have their holidays, on which they rest from work, he sometimes, albeit seldom, claps blinders on his ears and refrains from storing up the hearable things. This happens quite simply, he makes himself noticeable, he looks people in the eye, the things they say in these circumstances are quite unimportant and do not suffice to spell their doom. When he has taken off his secret ears, he is a friendly person, everyone trusts him, everyone likes to have a drink with him, harmless phrases are exchanged. At such times, people have no inkling that they are speaking with the executioner himself. It is not to be believed how innocent people are when no one is eavesdropping.

The Loser

He succeeds in losing everything. He starts with little things. He has a lot to lose. There are so many places where you can do a good job of losing.

The pockets he has specially made. The children who run after him on the street shout "Mister" here, "Mister" there. He smiles delightedly, and never bends over. He refuses to find anything, not on your life. No number of people running after him could make him bend over. He has lost what he has lost, and why did he take it along in the first place? But how can so many things still remain with him? Don't they run out? Are they inexhaustible? They are, but no one understands. He seems to own an enormous house full of tiny objects, and it seems impossible to get rid of all of them.

Perhaps fully loaded cars drive up to the back door and unload while he goes out to lose. Perhaps he does not know what happens while he is gone. He doesn't trouble himself about it, it doesn't interest him; if there were nothing left to lose, he would certainly gape in wonder. But he never found himself in such a situation, a man of uninterrupted losses, a happy man.

Happy, for he always notices it. One could think he does not notice at all, one could think he is sleepwalking and does not realize he is walking and losing, it happens by itself, uninterruptedly, all the time, but no, that is not the way he is, he really has to sense it, he senses every little thing, otherwise it is no fun, he has to know that he has losses, he has to know it constantly.

The Bitter-tangler

The bitter-tangler bears her heavy clew, she never parts with it, she always has it in her possession, it is so heavy that she can barely lug it along, it keeps getting heavier. She has always carried it as long as she can remember, it never occurs to her that she could get rid of it. She is deeply bowed, she arouses pity in some people, but she fiercely resists all who pity her. These poor people have no inkling how badly off they are, no inkling of what lies ahead of them. She approaches them and looks askance at them, she senses their ominous misfortune from below. She knows it instantly, there is no remedy; whatever happens, it can only get worse, it gets more and more awful from one encounter to the next. She nods and thinks of her clew. All of them are entangled in it, she has a hard time, but they have a harder time.

The bitter-tangler likes to do good and says: Be careful! If only they listened to her. Do not walk under trees, she says, there are rotten branches. Do not cross any street, there are vicious cars. Do not walk along buildings, bricks fall from rooftops. Never shake hands or enter any home, they all teem with bad bacteria. The sight of pregnant women arouses her despair: do not have babies, she says, if they do not die at birth, then they die later. There are so many diseases, there are more diseases than babies, and they all pounce upon the poor little thing and why should it suffer so dreadfully. It is better off not coming into the world at all.

47

The bitter-tangler has never carried a child herself, that is why she can say those things. She has never trusted a man, she promptly looks away when a man looks at her like that. She has sewn for people, but that too is uncertain. She has known people who were dead before her sewing was done. The payment could not be gotten from them. But she does not complain. She puts it into the clew. She relies on it, everything is true in it; it happens just as it lies in the clew.

The bitter-tangler sleeps standing in a forgotten dead-end street. The clew is her bed and her pillow. She is cautious and does not give her name. She has never accepted a letter. Letters always contain some misfortune. She watches the mailmen astonished, they carry nothing but misfortune around and the stupid people read it.

48

The Fun-runner

The fun-runner would once have come with the wind, now he comes faster. No sooner has his airplane landed in Bangkok than he checks the take-off times for Rio and instantly makes a mental reservation for Rome. The fun-runner lives in the tempest of towns. There is something to buy everywhere, there is something to experience everywhere.

He enjoys living today, for what was it like in the past? Where did people really get to and how dangerous and bothersome traveling was! Now you can travel without the slightest effort. You name a city and you've already been there. Perhaps you get there again at some point; if it works out in the fun-runner, then anything is possible. People believe that he's been everywhere, but he knows better. New airports are built, new airlines spring into life. Doddery old men may dream of calm ocean voyages, he hopes they have a good time in their deck chairs, but that's nothing for him, he's in a hurry.

The fun-runner has his own language. It consists of names of cities and currencies, exotic specialties and clothes, hotels, beaches, temples, and nightclubs. He also knows where a war happens to be taking place, that can be bothersome. But if you're near it, life can be extremely wild, and if it's not too dangerous, he gets woolly, he goes to see the war for two or three days, and then hurries off somewhere else for contrast, where there is the opposite of war.

The fun-runner has no prejudices. He finds that people are alike everywhere, for they always want to buy something. Whether it's clothes or antiques, they crowd into shops. There is money everywhere, even if it's different, it is exchanged everywhere. Just show him a place anywhere in the world without manicurists and slums. If it doesn't take too long, then nothing human is alien to him, he feels sympathy for and interest in everything. A fun-runner who is not interfered with has no ill-will towards anyone; the world would be a much better place if everybody were like him. Everybody will be like him, but it is better to live in the meantime. The mass fun-runner will be no picnic. He sighs quickly, forgets all about it, and hops the next plane.

The Moon Cousin

A dream revealed to the moon cousin that she has relatives on the moon. She had already sensed it, for she had never come to a country without bumping into people who looked familiar, whom she appeared to have met earlier. They were not friends, she had never seen them before, nor did one understand their language. It was something in their looks: the way they bent their heads, the curve of the fingernails, the expectant stance of the feet. They felt drawn to one another before they even noticed these details. Suddenly, on the bustling main square of an exotic town, a man loomed before her, standing out from all the others. He strode towards her so confidently, as if they had parted only yesterday. He was staring at her unmistakably, he had noticed her too among all the others; and although mistakes can happen, it is not very likely for two perfect strangers, who have never met before, to make the same mistake at the same time. And one can soon establish that there are no ulterior motives, for if the sudden stranger wants nothing from you and is merely yielding to his pure amazement, if you see that he is going through the same thing you are, then it has to mean something.

The moon cousin never lets a sudden stranger go, whether male or female, though she prefers women, since it is better to avoid misunderstandings, which can easily lead to disappointments. You make an effort and usually you find a third lan-

51

guage to communicate in, the two of you sit down and exchange backgrounds, and soon the seeming gap shrinks. People have wandered a great deal in this world and have left their native lands for countless reasons. The earth is small, that is well-known today; distances are unimportant. The two of you have already come to a name that means something to both of you, and with a little patience and a lot of tact, it turns out—how unbelievable—that you both belong to the same family and perhaps even had an inkling of the other person's existence. If you have an instinct for it, if you keep your eyes and your memory open, then you don't need to court strangers, for you have relatives everywhere.

"I'm keeping a log," says the moon cousin, "and that's the only reason I travel. I've never been to any country in which I didn't find relatives. The world can't be as bad as people say. Why don't all people look for their families? Instead of going to strange lands to be a stranger there, you should travel in order to feel at home."

She has proven the truth of her presentiment and so she feels fine wherever she is, for the first thing she does upon arriving somewhere is to establish her family. She finds her bearings even in the smallest countries, and even if there were no more than ten people in a country, you can bet your life she'd be related to one of them.

When the first trip to the moon was being prepared, she was concerned about sending along a message for her moon cousin. She convinced one of the pilots how important it was to use this contact and he promised he would deposit her letter the first thing upon landing. It is not yet certain whether it

52

reached her cousin. But anything is possible, and the moment it turns out that her instinct has once again not been deceived, then "moon cousin," as people have mockingly nicknamed her, will become her honorific name.

The Home-biter

The home-biter has an ingratiating manner and knows how to form new friendships. He is especially popular with ladies, whose hands he kisses. Never getting too close for comfort, he bows, takes the hand like a precious object, and brings it the long way to his lips. A special curve makes the way longer, and he succeeds in arousing a sense of the lady's unattainability no matter how experienced she may be. Regretfully, he lets the hand go, and when it finally and very slowly glides out of his fingers, one can feel the sadness of his renunciation and one wishes to honor him.

Something like that is not forgotten, and thus the home-biter receives the loveliest invitations: some people who are giving a housewarming simply have to have him. He brings along the fragrance of old times. He is introduced at length to all the ladies and kisses hands each in its turn. Inconspicuously, obvious only to the connoisseur, the ladies line up; supposedly, some, who have already had their turn, join the end of the line again. However, the home-biter makes sure that he finishes, for that is not the reason he has come.

The home-biter looks for a room in which to be alone. It should not be too small, nor too out of the way, the air and the sounds of the celebration must be felt here too. It is important for him that the door remain open during the performance of his action. There has to be something costly in the room: a tapestry, a brocade curtain, a statue, a painting. He has never been to this house before, but he has had a good look around. He keeps his eyes open even when kissing hands.

The home-biter never visits someone's home without biting off a piece of it. He should not be left alone. He never knows beforehand what he is going to bite off. It just happens. It most likely depends on the lady of the house. Every hand that he brings to his lips moves him in a peculiar way, but the matter is clinched by the lady of the house. He takes along what he has bitten off as a keepsake. He cannot go away without biting something off. If nothing else turns up, he is satisfied with a buckle.

Until now it has always worked for him, and he has never been caught. He cannot stand interferences; if he has to let go of something that was already in his teeth, he flies into a rage and scorns it. He will not snap at it a second time, it has become rancid for him. The trick is to get away from the women who would like to follow him. But there is something about him that commands respect, and no one gets too familiar with him. People merely wonder about him and are curious about the women in his life. When he returns to the party satisfied, he's got it in his pocket.

The Bequeathed Man

The bequeathed man has always lived where he was needed, and he wants to remain needed. There are moments when he does not know to whom he belongs, he then waits for wills to be read. As soon as it is clear who has inherited him, he makes himself irreplaceable. He can do arithmetic for instance. He can speak languages. He can buy train tickets. He can change money. He never says no, never in his life—he is not so young anymore—has he ever said no. Saying no goes against his grain. He guesses wishes before is owners have them. He is a good observer. One could believe that he is inside his owner and observes him from within. Whoever it may be, he feels no distinctions, he feels wishes.

The bequeathed man was never sick, that would not do. Nor has he ever been asked. He has legs and arms, nobody notices them. He never speaks at home, only when he is out on an errand; he mutely brings the thing back, mutely puts it down, with prices, hours, messages, or other data in writing, and has already vanished again. No one has ever been in his room, it may exist, but if it does, he is hardly ever there, for he is up and about before anyone in the owner's family awakes, and he goes to bed later than anyone in the owner's family.

The bequeathed man never asks for a reference and would never have received one. There is never any question of salary;

since he never goes anywhere for himself, he does not need any. He does eat, but in moderation and without disturbing anyone. No one has ever seen him with his mouth open, he is tactful enough to attend to this quietly in a corner. Stealthily he touches his teeth and still has a few. He already knows when he is needed for traveling and buys himself a ticket of his own accord in the appropriate class. He translates foreign languages fluently, one is absolutely astonished at hearing him speak in foreign countries, since he is mute at home. He is frequently photographed on trips and occasionally, if he does not jump aside quickly enough, he is a sudden intruder in the picture. The owner's family looks and makes faces. One can rely on him even at such moments. He himself takes the films to be developed, and when he brings back the prints, he has vanished from them. How he does it is a mystery, he is not asked and does not explain it, the important thing is that the owner's family is not intruded upon and the bequeathed man does not appear anywhere.

The Wile-catcher

The wile-catcher looks around corners and will not be deceived. He knows what is hidden behind innocent masks, he knows, as if lightning had struck him, what someone wants from him; and before the mask falls of its own accord, he makes a quick decision and tears it off.

The wile-catcher can also bide his time. He goes among people and studies them, everything is significant. A person need merely crook his little finger to reveal his dreadful design. Everyone is after the wile-catcher, the world teems with murderers. If someone looks at him, he quickly averts his eyes, the man must not realize that he is unmasked. Let him lull himself a bit in his predatory lusts and hatch his diabolical plans undisturbed. For a time, the wile-catcher does not mind being thought a sucker. Meanwhile, he starts boiling, and he boils so hard that he could go up in steam. But he makes sure it does not happen, and he strikes before things come to that pass.

The wile-catcher collects evil designs. He has enough space and he keeps them well and calls his pocket, which is full of wiles, Pandora's Box. He walks softly in order not to frighten masks prematurely. If he has to say something, it sounds gentle, he speaks slowly as though it were difficult for him. If he looks someone in the eye, he thinks about somebody else as a diversionary tactic. If he makes an appointment, he shows up at the wrong time, much too late, as though he had forgotten it. He thereby lulls the enemy into false security, the enemy has time to form a wrong image of him. Then he shows up, apologizes humbly, and offers a hair-raising excuse for coming late; under the table the villain is already rubbing his hands. The wile-catcher then lets him speak for a long time and says nothing, he nods his head frequently as a sign of agreement, gazes stupidly and admiringly, is amazed and laughs and lets out some praise now and then. So far, everyone has been taken in by him. The wile-catcher takes his leave, gives the scoundrel his hand, shakes heartily, says ingenuously "I'll think it over," and starts off for home in order to arrange and systematize the wiles, of which none has eluded him.

He has a special gift for systems. After all, everything in the world has a system, nothing is fortuitous, every villainy is connected to all the others, basically it is one and the same blackguard who, for sham, disguises himself as many. The wile-catcher reaches in with his sharp mind, he clutches a whole dense tangle and pulls it out, holds it high and secretly feels sorry for the Creator, who worked so cleverly, and yet not cleverly enough to fool him.

The Defective

The defective keeps examining herself, on and on, and always comes across new defects. She nitpicks on her skin, locks herself up with it, and never tackles more than a tiny area at one time. She examines it with magnifying glasses and tweezers, she peers, pricks, and tries the same place several times. For something that appeared intact at the first examination turns out to be defective at the very next one. When she first began, after a deep disappointment, she did not realize how many deficiencies she had. Now she is covered with them and is still far from knowing them all. Once she has discovered one, she makes a mental note of it and examines it painstakingly when its turn comes again.

The defective suffers greatly from her knowledge about herself; after all, nothing ever improves. Once she has found something, it never changes, it remains and can be found over and over again. It is good that there is so much left to explore, for if she were done with her entire skin, she would be bound to collapse under the weight of her knowledge, she is kept upright by the realization that there is so much still to do.

It is a task that would drive some people to despair. But she enjoys it, for she lives for her own truth. She speaks to no one about it, whose business is it anyway, and she would like to be done with it before dying. As for doing her back, she dare not think about it. She is leaving it for last and hopes for some inspiration enabling her to examine her back.

The defective dreams that her skin is being flayed off, every tiny spot, the whole skin, and hung up secretly for her in the attic. There, where the wash is hung for drying, the skin could be kept quite inconspicuously; if it were done right, no one would notice. That would make some things easier. The problem of the back would be solved and you could proceed more calmly and more justly. The work would be more even and you would not always have the feeling that this part or that were taking exception to your dwelling on the other parts.

The defective suspects that all women secretly do the same thing. For once a woman has really looked at her skin, how can it ever give her any peace again? That is why it itches, that means it wants to be looked over and taken seriously. The defective envies no one, she knows what's what, she is not taken in by a radiant face, other areas look entirely different, she is astonished that men can be deceived and marry without an utterly meticulous examination, which would have to last years and years.

The Archeocrat

The archeocrat will not settle for less than millennia and she finds them. Had her grandmother been like her, she would have been satisfied with Troy, but that is over with. Progress is going back further, she is utilizing it. People dig and dig, and she knows where. Nothing remains concealed from her. She carries the most ancient gold, no one may touch it, it was meant for her even back then; when those utterly ancient cities perished, they knew for whom they were perishing. The dousing rod she carries in her heart tells her where the earth was populated.

She makes fun of lower natures that push into jewelry shops and determine the value of precious objects by prices. Things that can be purchased may be all right for the nouveaux-riches or other riffraff. The archeocrat knows what she owes herself, she has in her bones those ancient cultures in which it took years to polish a stone and slaves were made up of respectability, and patience.

She cannot be fooled by blood—it has been watered down by mixtures—one knows how people come into being, through which wretched chances, which pride is reliable, who will not sell himself; she refuses to track down her background, she would have to shake with disgust no matter what she found. The only things that are intact are those that have lain in the earth, and the more millennia they have lain there, the more intact they are. She can only smile at the hollow minds that bank on pyramids. Let no one pester her with a pharaoh, all mummies are false, she wants the real thing, which no one knows anything about, and the moment in which it is brought to light, that moment alone is the moment of truth.

A few days later, the swindlers pitch into it, and when the costly objects are polished to a high shine, they look contemporary.

The archeocrat tolerates no one around her and has no family. Guarded by alert but obedient dogs, she lives alone, except when traveling. But she is usually traveling. With her immense wealth, which she despises, she supports archeologists all over the world, and, when something has happened, she has to be on the spot to make sure of her statutory portion before it becomes common and public and lands in the museums, where it vanishes for all time.

The Horse-dark Woman

The horse-dark woman has learned little and does not get along with people. She does not lack for words, she reads and writes, but when a person talks to her and expects an answer, she is tongue-tied. The very fact that someone is standing before her, gazing at her, the very fact that lips are opening before her and shaping sounds, robs her of the courage to react as a biped, any vis-à-vis terrifies her.

She then turns away and, evasively shifting her eyes, she trembles, her eyes fill with tears. She is ashamed of all words that other people speak so easily. Why doesn't anyone come before her and hold his tongue? Perhaps she could gradually get used to a confrontation. Perhaps she could prepare herself for words that have not yet been spoken. But no one grants her the time. Someone comes over to her, he is already standing there, he is already looking at her, he is already opening his mouth and speaking. Before she even dares to look him in the eye, she is assaulted by words, if they at least were soft, unusual words, words such as she carries secretly inside herself—but they are always gross and pointed formulas, that patter on her face like hard, small stones and injure it.

The horse-dark woman seeks refuge with horses in stables. She places herself next to an animal and calms herself on its smooth flanks. Not a word is spoken, tails amiably beat to and fro, ears perk up, recognizing her presence, nostrils quiver. Eyes turn towards her silently, she has no qualms about looking into eyes that offend no one.

The horse-dark woman is glad that she is not a horse herself. She does not wish to be anything that she views as her peer. She is comfortable only with what is always alien. She does not ingratiate herself, she does not fondle, she has no sounds of her own; and she wishes to be understood as little as she would like to understand. The darkness in which she has to live is something she finds only among horses. She has never tried anything with animals that want to be closer to her. It would be an error to believe that she likes to ride horses. But she finds her way into stables, which sometimes exist, she finds the time when they are deserted by people, and she remains only as long as no one is expected.

The horse-dark woman is not suffering from an excessive love for herself, but with horses she can be alone.

The Paper Drunkard

The paper drunkard reads all books, no matter what, so long as they are hard. He is not content with books that are being talked about; they have to be rare and forgotten, and hard to find. On occasion, he has been forced to spend a year hunting down a book because no one knew it. Once he finally has it, he reads it quickly, catches on, and can always quote from it. At seventeen, he looked the way he looks now at forty-seven. The more he reads, the more he stays the same. Any attempt to surprise him with a name goes awry; he is equally well-versed in every area. Since there is always something left that he does not yet know, he has never been bored. But he makes sure never to let on what he does not know, so that no one else will read about it first.

The paper drunkard looks like a box that has never been opened so that nothing can get lost. He shuns speaking about his seven doctorates and mentions only three, it would be child's play for him to acquire a new doctorate every year. He is friendly and likes to talk; in order to be able to speak, he lets others have their say. When he says "I do not know," one may expect a detailed and knowledgeable lecture. He is fast, for he is always seeking new people to listen to him. He never forgets anyone who has listened to him, the world is made for him of books and listeners. He knows how to appreciate the silence of others, he himself is silent only briefly before launching into a lecture. Actually, no one wants to learn from him because he knows about so many other things. He generates disbelief, not because he never repeats himself, but because he never repeats himself with one and the same listener. He would be entertaining if it were not always something different. He is fair to his knowledge, everything counts, people would give a great deal to stumble upon anything in him that counts more than something else. He apologizes for the time in which he sleeps like ordinary people.

You are filled with expectation upon seeing him again after many years, and you long to finally catch him in the act of cheating. But your longing is in vain—even though he speaks about totally different things, he is exactly the same down to the very syllable. Sometimes he has gotten married in the interval, sometimes he has been divorced. The wives disappear, it was always a mistake. He admires people who provoke him to outdo, and when they are outdone, he junks them altogether. He has never been to a city without first reading everything about it. Cities adjust to his knowledge; they confirm what he has read about them, unreadable cities appear not to exist.

He laughs from afar when a moron approaches. A woman who wants to marry him has to write him letters asking for information. If she writes often enough, he becomes hers and wishes to have her questions around all the time.

The Tempted Woman

The tempted woman cannot go outdoors without being pursued by men. She has not even taken three steps—and they have already noticed her and are following her, some cross the street for her. She hasn't the foggiest notion what causes it, is it the way she walks, but she can't find anything out of the ordinary in the way she walks. She doesn't look at anybody, if she at least provoked men with a look. . . . . She is not dressed in any conspicuous manner, she has no special perfume—elegant, that's what she is, elegant and distinguished, and her hair—could it possibly be her hair? She did not pick her hair, but she wears it in an unmistakable way.

She only wants to be left in peace, but she does have to get a breath of air and you can't always avoid going outdoors. Sometimes she pauses in front of a shop window and she can already see someone in the glass, he is standing behind her about to annoy her, and, that's right, he speaks to her. She doesn't even listen, she can imagine what that man is saying, and she doesn't answer him on the spot, that would be doing him too big a favor. But if a man becomes such a pest that she can't get rid of him, she suddenly turns to him and angrily hisses right into his face, so close that her hair brushes his tie: "Just what do you want from me? I don't know you! Stop pestering me! I'm not that sort of woman!"

What do they expect? Why don't they believe her? She doesn't really look, she doesn't even know what those men look like. But her words do not fail to have their magical effect, he becomes an even bigger pest, perhaps it's the effect of her hair on his tie. She has to tell him as close up as possible, to avoid attracting attention. Otherwise what would people think if they heard her angry words? But he carries on as though she were that sort of woman and he runs his hand over her hair. If it weren't for the people around them, she'd have slapped his face by now. However, the tempted woman knows what is proper for her to do, she swallows her anger and escapes to the nearest shop window. If she doesn't get rid of him now, she silently lets him come along from window to window, she doesn't grant him even one more syllable, and she makes extra sure that his tie doesn't get too close again. At last, discouraged, he lets up. But the tempted woman is still waiting for a man to say: "Excuse me, please, I see that you are not that sort of woman."

The tempted woman is a woman with self-respect, she cannot afford to do without window displays. She changed her perfume to be left in peace, it does not help. She even dyes her hair a different color, she has gone through all colors, but men still always want the same thing from her, they are all after her, she needs a knight to protect her from those men, where can she find one?

The Tired Woman

The tired woman sits in her restaurant and watches out. She is no longer young, she is not all that old either, but old enough to sigh over too much work. She greets the steady customers entering the place. As the owner or as the owner's wife, whichever, she has the right to be asked how she feels. "How are you today?" "Tired," she says, whether it is twelve noon or twelve midnight, and not without giving reasons for her tiredness. If it is noon, she says: "I worked eighteen hours yesterday"; if it is midnight: "I worked eighteen hours today." This sentence is the only thing that does not tire her, she has been reiterating it for years a hundred times a day. She accompanies it with a weepy face, stands up to show how close she is to collapsing, takes two steps, and really does collapse. She makes sure she falls upon a cushioned seat, she does not want to get hurt if she does collapse. As soon as she is properly seated, she casts beseeching glances around her and says: "Tired."

But a waiter has already done something wrong: failed to notice a guest, forgotten something in a dish. She flares up and starts yelping and screeching away in her language, and keeps yelping and yelping tirelessly. The cross she wears on her chest is affected by her excitement, it dances nastily to her words. All her sentences end shrilly on a very high note. Since there are many sentences, every conversation stops, no one can

70

understand his own words anymore, the patrons go mute. Loving couples are seized with anxiety about their future and they no longer look into each other's eyes.

Scolding, she gets up from her seat, staggers to the counter, personally takes hold of a plate, staggers through the restaurant, changes her mind, and carries the plate back to the counter, where, amid the shrillest squawks, she deposits it without smashing it. No one dares to order anything, who could possibly wish for anything except her silence? New customers may come, the tired woman nods by way of greeting and keeps scolding unswervingly. She yelps to make sure that everything is in order, that's why she's there after all, the cross on her chest gives her strength, without the cross everything would be over after three sentences. When she finally collapses on her seat, she peers around, her eyes begging for pity, and whimpers: "Tired."

The Delayer

In the morning, the delayer goes down for his mail, looks at the outsides of his letters, and sorts them. He hides the urgent ones so effectively that they can never be found again. With less urgent ones he makes less of an effort. But all are done away with. No day begins without his taking care of his mail. Once it's gone, he breathes a sigh of relief and sets about forgetting. The safest thing is for him to go back to sleep after taking care of his mail. For when he wakes up again, he doesn't even know what mail there was: otherwise he would have to start changing the hiding places. It is not easy to forget so much at once.

The delayer looks at the clock to find out where he must not go, since someone is waiting for him. He seeks out quiet places, where nobody knows him, to spend the time in which someone wanted to pester him. The time passes very swiftly, because he cannot be found and he enjoys picturing the people who look for him. He is highly respected for his untraceableness. It is assumed that he is very busy, and since no one has found out what he is busy with, people are forced to believe that it is something very important.

The delayer avoids people who remind him of something. If someone does happen to remind him, he shrinks and says: "Was that really me?" He regards himself as free because nothing happens, for everything that happens has consequences. He is well-known because he lives so privately. The bell on his door has not been working for years. He would not dream of repairing it, and sometimes he secretly peeps from his window when people stand in front of his name plate and uselessly press the button. They can press and press, he does not hear them; the longer he watches them, the more content he is. When it is dark, later on, he stands outside the door himself and buzzes up to himself to enjoy the situation even more thoroughly.

He knows why he is leery of visitors, who walk on his carpets: thousands of unopened letters are lying under the carpets. The mattresses are so heavy with letters that he would be incapable of lifting them up. He has practically no empty valise left in the attic. Likewise, there is enough to read up in the closets. He avoids the bookcases, for every book that he pulls out is crammed with letters. He throws no letter away, for it might contain something important. It would be frivolous to get rid of a letter before knowing what is inside. A time might come when he would have to look for something. It eases his mind to recall that everything is there. So long as nothing has vanished, nothing is lost.

The Humility-forebear

The humility-forebear nestles with destiny, the inevitable is his bliss. It is useless saying no to the inevitable, so he says yes before it even knocks. He walks about somewhat bent, thereby proclaiming his willingness to bear any yoke. But he strives not to look around too much, to keep from being noticed by yokes. For each yoke wants to be borne in its own way; if there are too many, they lose their identity, and nothing is more dismal than routine.

The humility-forebear twists from one submission to another. He feels what good it does, he can rationalize it with deep-felt words. He is convinced that man exists for the inevitable: that is the very thing distinguishing him from the animals. *They* do not know, they are always fleeing, as though they could escape their destiny. Eventually they *are* eaten, and the poor things have no inkling that this is the way it has to be. Man, however, incessantly waits for his destiny and welcomes it.

"Do you want to live forever?" he says to his child after it has barely learned how to speak, and he prepares it at an early age for submission; let it become like him and not go through life blindly, let it increase the number of humility-forebears.

He knows that a person who is eager to die will practice submission early on, and the trick is to live in the teeth of this

74

insight. This trick consists in doing absolutely nothing against what must be. "And how can one distinguish what must be from other things?" One is born with an instinct for that, he says, and a man's wisdom consists in never losing that instinct.

One is well-advised never to hear about struggles for freedom, rebellions, uprisings, or even mere protests. If one does hear about them, however, one should go all the way and also learn how useless they were. Either they fail or they do not fail. If they do not, then everything remains as before. A man who sees everything and takes it as it is and always was will maintain his dignity. The worst is good if only it comes as destiny, for it is the hardest.

The humility-forebear practices bearing up under hardship. He does it so well that he is sometimes pricked by malice; then he succeeds in intercepting a hardship before it properly arrives. Thus one burden is supplanted by the other, he too has a sense of variety. Each new burden increases the sublimity of man.

The humility-forebear is bursting with experience. He scatters advice right and left. It is always the same.

The Sultan-addict

The sultan-addict, a woman, suffers from the disappearance of the harem. Those were men who understood something about women, they weren't forever satisfied with the same one. They had self-confidence, they had fire in their blood, they didn't cut themselves off for their work, they weren't totally obsessed with making money. Just look at these gentlemen who come home from their businesses to their monogamous lives. That indifference! That tedium! That wretched empty peace and quiet! It is as though women were nothing, just cooks or mothers. Any servant, any nurse could replace them. No wonder women's souls are being perverted, they don't even know their raison d'être. Some are actually brazen enough to go to work and to live just like their husbands: doing business, becoming unfeeling and self-important and cold, coming home at night equally tired; looking just like a man, wearing his pants, speaking his language, and content to prove themselves against men on the outside instead of against women at home.

The sultan-addict, who dreams about harems, feels sorry for Turkey, which has abolished what was once the greatness of the empire. So much for the conquests, so much for the grandeur, a land like any other, more modern than before, but oh so humble. As long as they had harems, the Turks were great, they had to wage wars to fill the harems up, all their conquests were out of lust for new women, how can one help loving them for that splendid insatiability! To feel upon oneself the eyes of a man for whom several wives and countless concubines are waiting! To know he is comparing you with those others, to be something very special arousing his interest, to hold your own in his eyes—a victory! Like his victories on the field of battle! To hold him, to offer him something that no other woman could offer him! To work with poison and eunuchs for her son's advancement, to strengthen her son's resolution to get rid of all his brothers and rivals!

The sultan-addict is disgusted by a world in which there is nothing truly feminine left to do. Should you become a movie star and have the very same chances as a man who does exactly the same thing that you do? Should you dance for an audience? Should you sing? Is there anything men do not do today? And are you supposed to be a woman just to emulate them? The one thing that only a woman can do is to bear a prince, who kills all the other princes and eventually the sultan too when the sultan gets too old.

The sultan-addict installs a harem for herself, locking herself up in it. There she remains forever, never leaving. There she wears transparent clothing as befits the place, and she practices intimate dances, only for him. There she waits for the sultan, who never comes, and she imagines that he is on the way to her. There he would find everything he is accustomed to and, as is suitable for him, there he would find it better. There she throws herself ardently at his feet and begs him for his most abominable desires.

The Allusive Woman

The allusive woman is reluctant to give anything of herself and is ashamed of everything, even words. She helps herself out by always saying something other than what she means and avoiding all direct words. She speaks in conditional clauses, in the subjunctive, she halts and makes a pause before every noun. She would feel better in the world if there were no bodies. She treats her own as if it did not exist. She notices it only when she has to cover it, but even then she manages not to make any contact with it. No one has ever heard her utter the name of any part of the body. Her art of circumlocution is highly developed, there are periods of literature in which she would have felt at home, but living today is a heavy cross. For everyone provokes her, everyone shocks her, no sooner do you look away than you spot something else, the best thing would be to look away incessantly in brief starts.

The allusive woman pleadingly says "please" before addressing someone, which means that this person should take pains to use her language, reply similarly, avoid anything that offends her, and not torment her—for it torments her greatly, from the very moment that people try to shake her hand—so she imploringly says "please" and holds back her hand. She can already feel the pressure even in a glove, which she would never remove, and her peace of mind is gone, for suddenly her own body is there along with the other person's body, and she is so embarrassed she could sink into the ground.

"Please!" she says, then comes one of the sentences which only she understands, and worst of all she has to repeat it. She is stared at as though speaking in a perfectly foreign tongue, then she does not know which is more unbearable, staring eyes or frank words.

The allusive woman has to go shopping for she lives alone. Her needs have shrunk down to a minimum, she knows about things that she could not buy no matter what, since they have horrible names. She does go hungry, but she must not fall ill, for there are devils in the world who are known as physicians and who ask you straight out where it hurts.

The God-swanker

The God-swanker never has to ask himself what is correct, he looks it up in the Book of Books. There he finds everything he needs. There he has a moral support. There he leans, assiduous and powerful. Whatever he plans to do, God will endorse it.

He finds the sentences he needs, he could find them in his sleep. He does not have to worry about contradictions, they stand him in good stead. He skips anything not useful to him and dwells on an indisputable line. He absorbs it for all time until, with its assistance, he has achieved what he wanted. But if life then goes on, he finds another sentence.

The God-swanker trusts the pluperfect and calls upon its help. The tricks and gadgets of the modern age are superfluous, you get along much better without them, they only make everything more complicated. Man wants to have a clear answer and a consistent one. A wavering answer is useless. There are different sentences for different questions. Let anybody give him a question to which he could not find a suitable answer.

The God-swanker leads a regular life and wastes no time. The world may cave in around him, but he has no doubts. He Who created the world will save it from destruction at the very last moment; and if it cannot be saved, He will rebuild it after the annihilation so that His Word may survive and be right. Most people shall perish because they do not heed His Word. Those, however, who do heed His word do not really perish. The God-swanker has been saved from every danger. Thousands have fallen all about him. But he is still alive, nothing has ever happened to him, doesn't that mean something?

The God-swanker, in his humility, takes no undue credit for it. He knows the stupidity of human beings and feels sorry for them, they could have such an easier time of it. But they do not wish to. They think they live in freedom and do not realize how greatly they are enslaved to themselves.

When the God-swanker waxes furious, he threatens them, not with his words. There are better words to scourge people. He then stations himself erect with a bloated voice-sack as though standing personally on Mount Sinai and thunders and threatens and spews and flashes and shakes the riffraff to tears. Why did they refuse to listen to him again, when will they finally listen to him?

The God-swanker is a handsome man, with a voice and a mane.

The Granite-cultivator

The granite-cultivator is a woman who does not care for excuses. Murderers try to excuse themselves too and they talk and talk until people forget that there is a murdered man. If *he* could talk, then the whole thing would look altogether different. Not that she feels sorry for murder victims, for how can a person possibly let himself be murdered? But then again, it is good that there are murder victims so that the murderers may be punished.

The granite-cultivator has her children pray at night: "Charity begins at home!" When they fight, she goads them on until they resort to violence. The thing she likes best is seeing them box: she cares little for harmless sports. Of course, she does not object when the boys swim. But it is more important for them to learn how to box.

They are to get rich and know how to make a million. But they are to feel no pity for the suckers who let themselves be cheated. There are two kinds of people: cheaters and cheated, weak and strong. The strong are like granite, no one can get anything out of them, you can squeeze all you like. It is best never to give anything. The granite-cultivator could have struck it rich, but then the children came. Now let the children get rich. Work is bad for the mind, she tells them every day. If you're smart, you let other people work for you. The granite-cultivator sleeps well because she knows that she gives nothing.

Her door stays shut. No man crosses her threshold. Men hang you up with kids and then forget to pay. And they're not very capable either, otherwise they wouldn't keep trying. If a man who has really made it were to come, she would certainly recognize him. But a man like that has no time and so he never comes. The loafers, they'd like to come.

The granite-cultivator has never wept. When her husband went to the dogs, she wouldn't forgive him. She has held it against him for eight years now, and when the children ask about him, she says: "Father was stupid. A moron like him goes to the dogs." The granite-cultivator does not view herself as a widow. Her husband, who was such a moron, does not count in her eyes, that is why she is not a widow. Men are totally useless anyway. They feel sorry for people and let others put one over on them. She does not give anything, no one takes anything away from her, men could learn by her example.

The granite-cultivator does not like to read, but she has harsh homilies. When something harsh is said to her, she hears it immediately and adds it to her harsh homilies.

The Stature-explorer

The stature-explorer compares and measures; he has his own standards. They change with time and occasion, there are statures that are willingly explored and others that balk at it. He has specific, incomparable questions, he also has small whips. A great deal depends on birthplaces, there are some that cannot be considered for statures, this may be due to the water. There are those that are always being left behind; then again, others overrun because their high rates of growth are known. The stature-explorer is incorruptible and has objective criteria. He pulls a ruler from his pocket, a compass, a scale, a sextant, he knows exactly what he's doing, he does it before you can say Jack Robinson, he computes and estimates, adds and subtracts, and all who do not measure up to his standards are scornfully cast aside.

The stature-explorer does not make things easy for himself, he torments himself to do his level best. But he also has boisterous moments. He hurls all the tools of his trade on the ground, flings both arms in the air, and shouts: "Genius!" At this point, there is absolutely nothing more to say. It is rumored that he does not enjoy measuring all that much and does it all merely to burst out unexpectedly and irrevocably with a genius. All explanations stop, even the best birthplace does not help, and even the worst cannot spoil a thing. The stature-explorer makes sure that the number of geniuses is not too large. Moreover, they have to be whole, it is quite wrong to come up with quarter- and eighth-geniuses. All ordinary ways of computing are useless here, perhaps integral calculus would help one along, but that too is questionable. The important thing is that the number of geniuses is limited in every century.

It is thus advisable not to produce any genius without compelling reasons. Some remain concealed for a long time, not everyone is endowed with a scent for them. Some are hidden deep underground. Only the stature-explorer himself possesses a divining rod and it may take a lifetime to spirit a dozen geniuses out from the past, in which they have holed up. The stature-explorer does have the stuff to be a genius himself, but he decided on his harder chore at an early time. He embodies the law of ethics, he is highly moral, and because theft ranks just behind murder, and geniuses unabashedly steal like magpies, he forgoes being one himself and is content to fathom their unfathomableness.

The stature-explorer achieves position and authority, no one deserves it as much as he, for without him humanity would be done for, no one would know where a genius has holed up, no one would know how to pull him out, polish him, and dust him, and remove the moral cinders adhering to him, no one would know how to proclaim him, how much light he needs, what to feed him, how to air him and how often, what enemies to keep him away from so that he won't explode, and no one would know when it was time again to shut him up.

85

The Starry Woman

The starry woman shuns the crude light of the sun. It is indiscreet, it is tactless, it is painfully bright; there is a great deal within, waiting for its moment, but it is ruthlessly yanked forth, spread out, lit up, and heated, until it is no longer to be recognized, just where was it really—in him, in her, in all?

The starry woman sticks to crystals, which cannot be opened. Even the transparent ones among them are certain of their hardness; and if you like to see a thing, you should not have it. The starry woman desires closure, on which weak and tested light falls. It may have found its way to her from the stars, but it knew nothing about her before finding her, and she listened in her reclusion for a long time until it came, and was herself uncertain and dark.

She has peered through a telescope only once in her life. How ashamed she was! She felt as if she were brazenly hurtling towards a star and forcing it to shine brighter than it cared to. She did not forget how lonesome it suddenly was, separated from the others, which gave it its stillness and equilibrium. She had plucked it out from all the heavens; her eye, ordinarily slow and quiet, glared at it, the way the sun glared at her in the daytime, she was afraid the star was destroyed now and lost from the sky. She tore herself away, she cursed the instrument, she did penance in her own way for weeks by making her eyes evade that cursèd star. Then, when she dared to seek it again and found it, she was so happy that she purchased the telescope of her shame, smashed it, and scattered the parts and splinters in the night.

The starry woman sighs in relief when the sun is gone and she wishes it would never come again. She spends her days in dark places. She works only to make the days go by. Her skin is as pure as the light of the sun. But she does not realize this for she does not see herself. She has never wasted a thought on herself. Her only mirror is the illuminated night, and this mirror consists of so many dots that it has no unity. Where can it start? Where can it stop? Can it be so clear without having seen itself?

The starry woman has thoughts, she keeps them to herself, she is afraid of losing them upon uttering them. But they do not freeze within her, they wax and wane, and when they have become so small again as to vanish from her, they awake in others.

The Hero-tugger

The hero-tugger potters around monuments and tugs on the trousers of heroes. They may be of stone or of bronze, but in his hands they come alive. Some get up in the middle of traffic, they had best be left alone. But the ones in parks are the very ones we need. He sneaks around them or else he lurks in the bushes. When the last visitor has gone away, the hero-tugger jumps out, heaves himself skillfully onto the pedestal, and stands next to the hero. He remains there awhile, mustering his courage. He is full of respect and does not reach in right away. He also thinks about where the best place would be. It is not enough to put his hand on a curve, he has to hold something in his fingers, otherwise he cannot tug: he needs folds. When he has one, he does not let go for a long time, he feels as if he had it in his teeth. He senses the greatness passing over to him and he shudders. Now he knows what he really is and what he could do. Now he makes up his mind again, now he tugs hard, now he glows with strength, he will begin tomorrow.

The hero-tugger does not climb any higher, that would be inappropriate. He could heave himself up to the stone shoulder and whisper something into the hero's ear. He could pull his ear and reproach him for various things. That would be the height of infamy. He contents himself with the modest place that is proper for him. He is still clutching folds in the trousers. But if he works hard, never misses a night, and keeps tugging more and more firmly, the day will come, the radiant day, when he will heave himself up with a powerful surge and, in front of the whole world, he will scornfully spit on the hero's head.

The Maestroso

The maestroso, if he moves forward at all, strides on columns. They are in no hurry, but they carry him well, and there is quite a bit to carry. Wherever the columns settle, a temple takes shape, and the worshipers are there in the twinkling of an eye. He lifts his stick and everyone is mute, he fills the air with measured signs. The worshipers remain silent, the worshipers meditate, the worshipers rack their brains about his signs.

In the pauses between his moments of sublimity, the maestroso feeds on caviar. There is little time, he will stand up again right away. But he does nothing alone, many people surround him and gaze at the caviar, which is meant only for him. The maestroso burps melodically.

The maestroso travels with solemn dignity around the world, all stones are cleared from his path, rocks, mountains, and oceans. He sits in his special compartment, all by himself, the adepts stand bare-headed in the corridor, while he has his musical score in front of him, marking with weighty strokes the things that only he may mark, and the others outside shudder at every stroke of his. The train halts when he rises, and it does not move on until he sits, the train never stops where he does not want it to, and for his sake it stops in the open countryside.

The maestroso leaves a wife behind in every temple, she waits for him as in olden times. There she sits and sits and is all his, with child and body and soul, and when he comes back on his columns, then even if years have not gone by, she shudders and stands praying among the others. He sees her but it is not the time to know her, a woman who has waited an eternity must practice a little more patience. But then, but then he nods to her, he has nodded to her among all the others, she would be willing to be burnt alive for this nod.

The maestroso knows that he will grow old, he knows the number of his years. If he was particularly satisfied with his performance, he arranges a celebration, at which the others may also sit and drink, but he never drinks the same beverages. Then he smiles—he has never laughed—and has each one come individually to him from the round. "Show your hand!" he orders and knowledgeably scrutinizes the lines. He tells the person how young he must die, he beckons to the next one.

The Thrown Woman

The thrown woman never awakes in the same bed, and she rubs her eyes. Where is she? She has never been here before! How did she get here? Who threw her here? She is amazed, but not for long, because she has her plans and does not care to lose her precious time solving riddles. She awakes, stretches, she spruces herself up, she does not yet know who will take care of her today.

One cannot say that she goes out hunting, she must be found. She has her places, where she is tolerated, and it never takes long, a very special man always comes over to her, he is good-looking and does something important, he has a special cut, either his suit or his hair. He noticed her long ago, for she is never the first to notice, she notices only men who have made up their mind to go over to her. Even before the first sentence—all it takes is a look, a certain tilt of the unusual head, a superior smile, half-hidden under the moustache, a barely raised hand, a noble forefinger, lips on the verge of opening in admiration—even before the first sentence she feels thrown and caught and carried and thrown again, and she feels faithfulness spreading throughout her body; she sees no one but him, today she will not see anyone else, she would rather be torn to bits than even notice anyone else. If fate ordains that two good-looking men, both of whom do something important, both with a special cut—either their suits or their hair—approach her at the same time, she feels thrown by both, is faithful to both, and will not favor one over the other.

Such evenings, if you like, are lost evenings, for both men stick to their guns, neither gives in, she makes sure that neither gives in; she never reaches the point of forgetting and no longer knowing where she is, she never reaches the point of really being thrown, and, in order to lose neither one, she keeps conversing with both of them all through the night. There is then no question of sleep any more than of being thrown; no matter where she may be, she knows where she is, it's really too bad, for both are worth it, but that's the way she is, and faithfulness, faithfulness is her middle name.

The Man-mad Man

The man-mad man is not mad about men per se, as one might think from his name, he is really keen on the qualities of men. He seeks these qualities, he appropriates them, he belongs to them. There is no boldness, there is no strength that he does not espy, track down, and swallow. Those who are defeated go unnoticed, for him the world is made up of winners.

The man-mad man gave his mother a lot of trouble when he tried to get out of her womb. He was not even four months old when he scratched and knocked from inside. Furious at his imprisonment, he pushed her back and forth, the poor woman was at sixes and sevens, she could not sleep, she could not sit, she staggered around, he gave her no moment of peace. When he finally appeared much too early, he bit her before he had teeth.

The man-mad man got into fistfights right and left as a child, he hit away at anybody who wanted anything from him. At fourteen, he vanished and was never seen again. Where could he be? His mother was not worried, he could take care of himself, as surely as he had bit her without teeth.

He had crossed the pond. He knew how to be alone and not share with anyone. He was drawn to people who were doing well, he overlooked people who were doing badly. At the first boxing match he attended, he learned what he needed. He yelled for the winner until his throat was hoarse. But the loser stood up and was not dead. When he saw that the man had not been killed and managed to reel away, he felt disgusted. Boxing was nothing. But there was something better: weapons. Shots kill, shots are in earnest, he took weapons to his heart, acquired a few, utilized them, and bought and sold them with increasing self-confidence and impudence.

The man-mad man became a millionaire while young. There were still wars here and there and men who fought. He looked at the wars himself; if the prospects were good, he equipped soldiers, he was generous and granted loans. On his map, points shone wherever things were happening. Then he grabbed his plane and arrived on time, he risked danger, concluded treaties, and flew off into the next war. He knew every mercenary leader in the world personally. He shunned convictions, that was something for weaklings. Anyone keen on hitting away and nothing else could count on him.

The man-mad man is certain that nothing changes. As long as there are men worthy of the name, they will start hitting away at one another. After all, everyone knows there are too many people, and men are supposed to get rid of the superfluous ones.

The Woe-administrator

The woe-administrator has seen a thing or two in his life and there are good reasons why he has monopolized all the woe in the world. Wherever any horror has taken place, he was there, he was involved. Others talk about it and feel sorry about it, but he experienced it personally. He does not talk, but he knows better. How poignantly he gazes whenever one of his catastrophes is mentioned.

It began when the *Titanic* struck an iceberg. He leaped overboard, he floated in the water for sixteen hours. He never lost consciousness for an instant, he saw one person after another vanish in the water and he was the very last to be rescued.

The woe-administrator has lost all he had six times. He has known poverty and hunger; and since he was not born with a silver spoon in his mouth, he had to make do with iron. He has always worked his way up again with iron energy. No sooner did he reach the top than he lost everything again.

The woe-administrator has had several happy marriages and ought to have grandchildren and great-grandchildren by now. But all the members of his family, without exception, were snatched away from him by fatal illnesses. He had to accustom himself. His first wife, whom he cared for the most, entered medical history as the last case of the plague in Europe. And he can tell you a thing or two about leprosy, which no one around here would think possible. It happened right before his eyes: two of his daughters and half a son died of leprosy. But that did not turn him into a Weeping Willy, he took it like a man. One can understand, however, that he is not very impressed by other people's woes. He complains about nothing, he takes it upon his shoulders, he holds his tongue and smiles. When others talk a blue streak, he does listen, but let no one expect him to open up to those people who live their lives in one great woe.

The woe-administrator has a gentle way of noticing contradictions in the misery tales of other people. He does not ask a lot of questions, he keeps listening, but suddenly he corrects a date. It is quite presumptuous of someone to dare relate something that the woe-administrator has personally experienced from beginning to end. A light quiver of sarcasm will then play about his lips. Nothing at all can be sensed in his words when he expresses his condolences. It is not really mere politeness, it is stamped by his deeper knowledge, but one can guess what he is thinking. He knows them well, those robbers, who would like to pilfer each of his woeful experiences.

Recently, however, he reached the end of his rope. The name Pompeii was dropped and a thief of extraordinary format tried to tell him about those events: tell him, who was in Pompeii on that single day and was the only one able to escape! He shut that man up snidely. He simply would not stand for it. He rose to his feet and, overcome by the memories of that day, visibly excited, but not without dignity, he left the company. It did him good to perceive the awe-filled silence of the others all the way to the door.

97

The Invented Woman

The invented woman never lived, but she exists and makes herself noticeable. She is very beautiful, but different for each man. Ecstatic descriptions of her are given. Some men emphasize the hair, others the eyes. But there are discrepancies about the color, from radiant golden blue to deepest black, the same holds for the hair.

The invented woman varies in size and has any weight. How promising the teeth, which she shows over and over again. Her breasts either shrink or swell. She walks, she lies down. She is naked, she is marvelously dressed. In regard to her footwear alone, a hundred different items of information have been gathered.

The invented woman is unattainable, the invented woman acts easy-going. She promises more than she keeps, and keeps more than she promises. She flutters, she tarries. She does not speak, what she says is unforgettable. She is choosy, she turns to everyone. She is as heavy as the earth, she is as light as a breath of air.

It appears questionable whether the invented woman is aware of her importance. That too is a topic of argument among her worshipers. Just how does she manage to make everyone realize: It's she. Granted, the invented woman has an easy time of it, but did she have an easy time of it from the beginning? And who invented her to the point of unforgettableness? And who spread her across the inhabited world? And who idolized her and who sold her off? And who scattered her across the lunar deserts before a flag appeared on the moon? And who shrouded a planet in thick clouds because it was named after her?

The invented woman opens her eyes and never closes them again. In wars, the dying on both sides belong to her. Ages ago, wars blazed up because of her, not today, today she visits men in wars and, smiling, she leaves them a picture.

The Never-must

The never-must will not be forced to do anything by anyone, just try. He will not listen to the right, he will not listen to the left, can he hear at all? He understands very well what you want from him, but he already shakes his head and shoulders before he understands it. In place of a backbone, he has a powerful *No!* more reliable than bones.

The never-must spits out. Orders whirl about in the air and even though a man may avoid them like the plague, something does remain in him after all. He has a special handkerchief for things like that, and before it's full of spit he burns it.

The never-must never goes to any window for service. Those barred faces nauseate him, you can't tell them apart. He'd rather go straight to vending machines, get what he needs from them, and save himself the nausea. Nor is he yelled at by them, and he doesn't have to beg and plead. He just throws in the coin when he feels like it, presses the button, gets what he wants, and overlooks what he doesn't.

The never-must hates having buttons on him, he adjusts everything loosely and wears no trousers. Ties are the devil's handiwork for him, just right for strangling. "I'm not going to hang myself," he says when he sees a belt, and he is amazed at the unsuspecting innocence of its wearer.

100

The never-must moves in knight's gambits and has no address. He forgets where he is in order not to say it. If he is stopped and asked where to find a street, he says: "I'm a stranger here myself." The trick is that he is not only a stranger here, the trick is that he is a stranger everywhere. At times, he has left a house without realizing that he has spent the night there. A knight's gambit is all it takes and he is off to the side, everything has a different name and a different look; instead of hiding, he leaps away.

The never-must speaks only if he absolutely must. Words exert a pressure on him, other people's words and his own. What a state one is in when one is alone after a conversation and all words repeat themselves! They do not stop, one cannot get rid of them, they squeeze and squeeze, you gasp for air, where can you escape from the words? There are some words that repeat themselves with terrible, diabolical stubbornness, while others gradually yield and seep away. One can elude that affliction only with premeditation: one simply does not say the words, one lets them sleep.

The never-must has finally discarded his name and will not let himself be named. He springs away on his chessboard, cunningly and easily, and no one can call him.